SUPERHEROES ASSEMBLE!

Steve Cole
Jo Cotterill

Pictures by
Bill Ledger

OXFORD
UNIVERSITY PRESS

OXFORD
UNIVERSITY PRESS

Great Clarendon Street, Oxford, OX2 6DP,
United Kingdom

Oxford University Press is a department of the University of Oxford.
It furthers the University's objective of excellence in research, scholarship,
and education by publishing worldwide. Oxford is a registered trade mark of
Oxford University Press in the UK and in certain other countries

British Library Cataloguing in Publication Data

Data available

9780192776099

1 3 5 7 9 10 8 6 4 2

Paper used in the production of this book is a natural, recyclable product
made from wood grown in sustainable forests. The manufacturing process conforms
to the environmental regulations of the country of origin.
Printed in China

Acknowledgements
Illustrations by Bill Ledger
Activities by Rachel Russ
Design by James W Hunter
Photo assets supplied by shutterstock.com, cgtrader.com, turbosquid.com.

CONTENTS

Helping your child to read

Before they start

- Talk about the back cover blurb. Ask your child to think about how Cam might get the new pupil to join Hero Academy.
- Look at the front cover. Ask your child whether they recognise any of the heroes. Talk about what powers they might have.

During reading

- Let your child read at their own pace – don't worry if it's slow. They could read silently, or read to you out loud.
- Help them to work out words they don't know by saying each sound out loud and then blending them to say the word, e.g. *g-l-ow-i-ng, glowing*.
- Encourage your child to keep checking that they understand what they're reading. Remind them to reread to check the meaning if they're not sure.
- Give them lots of praise for good reading!

After reading

- Look at pages 37 and 71 for some fun activities.

BLAST FROM THE PAST

Steve Cole

Pictures by
Bill Ledger

In this story ...

Jin
(**SWOOP**)

Jin has the power to fly. He once had a race with a jumbo jet ... and won! He can fly high enough to reach outer space!

Cam
(**SWITCH**)

Mr Trainer
(**TEACHER**)

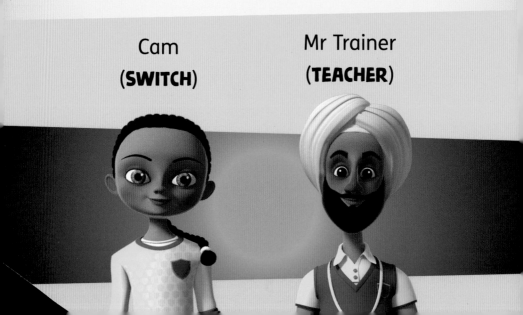

1
POWER CUT

Cam and Jin were studying in the library.
Mr Trainer was going to give them a test on
villains the next day.

   Cam was reading a book about some of
the worst villains in history. "Light Blaster
fired light beams at security guards to dazzle
them while he robbed banks," she read.

   "It's a good job he's locked up now,"
Jin replied.

LIGHT BLASTER

Catchphrase:
I'm having a blast!
Hobbies: collecting rare and unusual light bulbs.
Likes: fairy lights, disco balls.
Dislikes: power cuts, water.
Beware!
Light Blaster can use light to overpower his victims.

"At least Mr Trainer defeated Light Blaster," Jin said. "I wonder how he did it?"

"Why don't we ask him later?" Cam replied.

Cam and Jin didn't notice a glowing figure watching from behind a bookcase.

"Yes, I'd like to talk to Mr Trainer too ... " said the figure, softly.

Jin tried to read a couple more pages, but after a few minutes he gave up and put the book down. "We've been studying for ages," he said. "How about a game of Powerball?"

"You're on!" Cam replied.

The two friends walked to the sports hall and got a ball from the storeroom.

The rules of the game were simple: you had to kick the ball so hard it bounced off at least three walls, catch it with one hand and then hit a target.

An hour later, Cam and Jin were getting tired.

Suddenly, the lights in the sports hall **flickered** and went out.

"There must be a power cut," said Cam.

The emergency lights came on.

"We can still play one more game," said Jin, peering at Cam in the dim **glow**.

"I thought you were going to talk to Mr Trainer?" said a voice behind them.

Cam and Jin turned to see a glowing figure.

"**Light Blaster!**" gasped Jin.

2
BLAST BATTLE!

Cam and Jin stared in amazement at the person standing before them.

"He looks shorter than he did in the picture," Cam whispered to Jin.

"I'll bet he's still really DANGEROUS," Jin replied.

Cam took a deep breath and bravely stepped closer to the glowing figure. "I don't know how you got out of jail, **Light Blaster**," she said, "but you shouldn't be here."

"Hang on. I'm not—"

"**We're sending you back to prison!**" Cam said.

Cam turned to Jin and lowered her voice. "You'd better fly out of here and raise the alarm."

Jin took off at once. He *zoomed* up, spun round, then headed for the door, but Light Blaster was in the way.

"Stay back!" Light Blaster warned. The emergency lights grew dimmer, and Light Blaster GLOWED even more fiercely.

"Look out, Jin!" Cam called. "I think he's going to attack!"

POW! As Jin swooped over Light Blaster's head, he bounced off something invisible.

"Light Blaster must have created an energy shield," Cam thought in alarm.

Jin was flying out of control. "*Oof!*" He landed on a pile of crash mats.

"**NO!**" cried Light Blaster. "That wasn't supposed to happen!"

"I suppose you hoped for something worse," said Cam angrily. "Well, you won't get away with this."

Cam became Switch and shape-shifted into an owl.

As an owl, Switch could see clearly in the dim light. With a **_screech_**, she flapped into the air.

Light Blaster turned and ran from the sports hall.

As Light Blaster raced down the corridor, the lights around him **EXPLODED**. It was as if he was absorbing their energy. The energy **zapped** back out of him in blasts which hit the walls, lockers and windows.

Light Blaster flung open the doors and raced outside. "**Keep back!**" he yelled at Switch. "**I don't want to hurt you!**"

A blast of energy hit a nearby tree. Switch swerved out of the way as the tree trunk CRACKED and fell over, almost hitting her.

Switch frowned. If Light Blaster didn't want to hurt her, why was he doing this?

The caretaker's shed **EXPLODED** into splinters. Switch flew up higher to avoid the bits of wood. "I've got to stop this villain," she thought, "but how?"

3
FROM DARK TO LIGHT

Switch **swooped** down towards Light Blaster.

"**Keep away!**" he wailed. His **glowing** body was starting to **flicker** on and off. "I've absorbed too much energy. I can't hold it in much longer. I'm **dangerous!**"

Switch frowned. Was he telling the truth?
She flew closer to him. The hot CRACKLE
of his energy singed her wings.

Switch landed some way away and
changed back into Cam. "What will happen
if you release all that energy?" she called.

"It will explode in a massive blast of
power," said Light Blaster. "Please, help me!"

Cam thought for a moment, then made a decision. "All right, follow me."

Cam **charged** across the lawn as fast as she could, back into Hero Academy. Light Blaster followed behind, being careful to keep his distance.

Inside, Cam went straight to Mrs Molten's lab, where there was a special chamber to test out all new inventions. It was made of extra-tough glass and metal.

Light Blaster ran inside, throbbing with energy. Cam pushed the door shut behind him.

Cam stared at Light Blaster helplessly. What could she do?

Just then, Mr Trainer came running in with Jin. "What on earth is going on?"

"That's Light Blaster," Jin explained.

"He's stored up too much energy," Cam said. "We have to help him!"

Crackles of light **fizzed** off Light Blaster and bounced off the walls of the test chamber.

Mr Trainer strode forward and turned a dial on the outside of the test chamber. "This should do it," he said.

Cam heard a *whooshing* sound, like a vacuum cleaner, then some of the energy was sucked upwards into a vent.

"It's working!" Cam cried.

As more and more of the energy was drawn away, Light Blaster fell to his knees in relief.

"Who did you say that was?" Mr Trainer asked.

"It's Light Blaster. You caught him and put him in prison, remember?" Jin said.

Mr Trainer looked inside the test chamber, then frowned. "Actually I'm afraid it isn't."

Jin's face fell. "What do you mean?" he asked.

"Light Blaster is still firmly behind bars. Whoever this is, it isn't Light Blaster."

The door to the test chamber
creaked open.

"It's true," muttered a weak voice. "I'm
not Light Blaster. I'm his son ... **BLACKOUT**."

Cam and Jin gasped.

"I share some of Dad's powers," Blackout explained, "but I can't control them. I hoped that Hero Academy could help me. That's why I sneaked in … to see what it was like."

He looked at Cam and Jin. "I followed you two because I was hoping you'd lead me to Mr Trainer," Blackout continued. He turned to the teacher. "I thought you might be able to help me stop my powers."

"They don't need to be stopped, Blackout," said Mr Trainer.

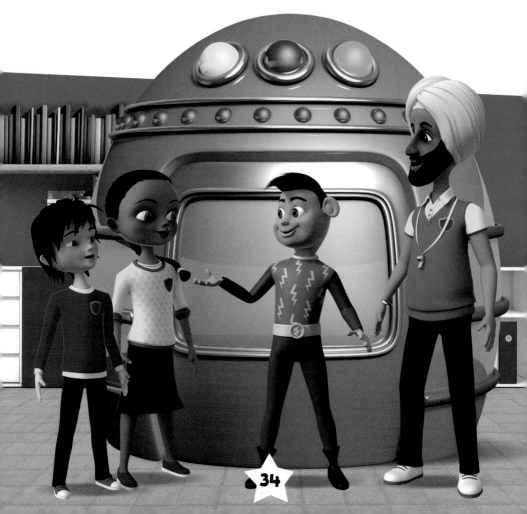

Blackout's eyebrows shot up in surprise. "What do you mean?"

"We can help you to control your powers," Mr Trainer said. "If you join Hero Academy, one day, you could be a superhero."

Blackout's face broke into a wide smile. "I would love that!" he said.

"I'll show you around," said Cam with a grin.

Blackout looked delighted. "That would be **awesome**!"

"Then it's settled," Jin declared.

"I think you'll do very well at Hero Academy, Blackout," Mr Trainer said. "In fact, I'm sure you have a very *bright* future ahead of you!"

AFTER READING ACTIVITIES

QUICK QUIZ

See how fast you can answer these questions!
Look back at the story if you can't remember.

1) What are Cam and Jin playing when the lights
   go out?

2) Who do Cam and Jin think Blackout is?

3) Where does Cam take Blackout?

THINK ABOUT IT!

How have Cam and Jin's feelings about the visitor to
Hero Academy changed by the end of the story?

POWERING BLACKOUT

Which of the following things do you think could help
to power Blackout?

CODE RED!

Jo Cotterill

Pictures by
Bill Ledger

Cam
(**SWITCH**)

Cam has the power to turn into different animals. She once stopped some baddies from robbing a bank by turning into a giraffe.

Axel
(**INVISIBOY**)

Pip
(**BOOST**)

Nisha
(**NIMBUS**)

Slink
(**COMBAT CAT**)

1
HATS

"I can't do it," Axel said, thumping his book down on the bench. "I just can't remember all this stuff. It's too hard."

"I know tests are scary," Cam told him, "but you're not going to fail. I know you can do it."

The two friends were sitting in the gardens of Hero Academy. They were studying for the Hero Academy Tests, or HATs, the most important tests of the year.

"When I'm feeling worried," Cam said, "I close my eyes and breathe very slowly. Then I count to ten. When I open my eyes, I feel much better."

Axel nodded. "I'll try to remember that."

"You just need to relax," Cam added.

"You're right," said Axel, picking up his bag.

"I think I'll go and play a game of Powerball. Are you coming?"

"Maybe later," Cam replied.

As Axel walked away, Cam saw Mr Trainer coming along the path towards her.

"Good work, Cam," said Mr Trainer.
"I overheard you talking. You showed
great hero qualities there."

Cam got to her feet. "I wasn't even using
my powers!"

"Yes you were. Superpowers aren't
always things like invisibility or flying."
Mr Trainer smiled. "By the way, the Head
would like to see you."

"Does he have a mission for
me?" Cam asked, excitedly.

"Why don't you go and find
out?" replied Mr Trainer.

2
THE NEW MISSION

Cam knocked on the Head's door and entered. She was surprised to see Slink sitting in the chair by the Head's desk.

"Hello, Slink!" said Cam. "I thought you were out looking for new superheroes to join the academy."

"He's just got back," the Head said, appearing from the holo-projector on his desk. "In fact, that's why I sent for you."

SLINK

Catchphrase: Meow!

Hobbies: sleeping, eating.

Likes: Scrummy-Yums cat food, being stroked just behind his right ear.

Dislikes: being woken up suddenly, running out of Scrummy-Yums.

Slink is no ordinary cat. He finds children with superpowers and then reports back to the Head. When he has found a new hero, the red lights on his collar turn green.

Slink can turn into Combat Cat and is a martial arts expert.

"I have a new mission for you," the Head continued, "but it could be very difficult."

Cam stood up straight. "I **can do it**," she replied confidently.

"Slink has found a potential pupil," the Head said. "A boy with strong powers. We want him to come to Hero Academy."

An image appeared on the screen behind the Head. It showed a boy with brown hair, standing in the middle of a bedroom. He looked very unhappy.

"This is Neo," said the Head. "He has water powers, but he can't control them yet. He used to go to **Superpower School** ..." The Head's voice grew sharper as he named the rival school. "He ran away and went back home, and now Neo says he'll never go to school again. I've offered him a place here, but he won't come."

"Poor Neo," said Cam, looking at the picture of the miserable boy. "What do you want me to do?"

The Head smiled at her. "This mission needs someone with special powers."

"Shape-shifting?" asked Cam.

"No, not shape-shifting," said the Head. "What Neo needs more than anything is a **friend**. You're a good listener. I'd like you to persuade Neo to come to Hero Academy. Slink will show you where he lives."

"I'll do my very best, sir," said Cam.

3
NEO

Later that day, Cam and Slink set off, leaving the academy through the secret door and entering an ordinary street. From the outside, no one would guess that there was an entire school behind Door 62!

Cam became Switch and shape-shifted into a cat, so she and Slink were able to cross rooftops and fences together. Soon, they reached Neo's flat, which was on the edge of Lexis City.

Cam changed back into her human form and rang the doorbell while Slink settled down next to a pot plant in the hall for a quick catnap.

The door opened, and Neo stood in front of Cam. "Hello?" he said, in an uncertain voice.

Cam smiled. "Hi. I'm Cam, from Hero Academy. May I come in?"

Neo frowned. "I already told them, I'm not going. **You can't make me!**" He started to close the door.

"**WAIT!**" said Cam. "Please. I didn't come here to make you do anything. I came because I thought you might need a friend."

Neo hesitated. "A friend?" he said.

"Who's at the door?" called a man, from further inside the flat.

"It's a girl from the other school," Neo called back. He turned to Cam. "You'd better come in, but we'll need to be quiet. Dad does shift work at the dam. He sometimes sleeps during the day."

Cam followed Neo into the flat. "Are you sure you won't think about coming to the academy?" she asked.

"I'm **not going!**" Neo said through gritted teeth. As he spoke, water sprayed out of his hands and soaked the floor in front of them. "Now look what you made me do!"

"I'm sorry," said Cam. "I didn't mean to upset you."

"No, I'm sorry." Neo looked away. "I've never been very good at controlling my powers," he said in a muffled voice. "The kids at my last school used to laugh at me."

"How horrible of them," said Cam. "But my friends aren't like that. There's Pip: she's super strong and super helpful. Nisha can control the weather, and she's really funny. Axel can turn invisible. He's really kind and a bit shy …"

Cam told Neo all about life at Hero Academy and all about her friends. As she talked, Cam noticed that the water from the drenched floor began to lift up in tiny droplets. The droplets drifted back towards Neo in a line. He turned his hands upwards, sending them spinning in a spiral above his head.

"**That's beautiful,**" said Cam, looking at the watery spiral.

Neo looked at his hands in surprise.

The water droplets fell from the air and **splattered** on to the carpet.

"See?" he said bitterly. "I can only do it if I'm not thinking about it. I'm a **failure**."

A mobile phone rang suddenly, making them both jump. Cam heard Neo's dad's voice from the other room. Then the bedroom door was flung open and Neo's dad rushed out, reaching for his high-vis vest.

"I have to go," he said.

"What's happened, Dad?" asked Neo.

"Can't stop," said his dad. "It's a **CODE RED!**"

Neo's dad threw on his high-vis vest and ran out of the front door.

Neo and Cam hurried to the window. A minute later, they heard a car start up and saw Neo's dad drive away.

4
EVERYONE IS IN DANGER!

"What's a Code Red?" asked Cam.

Neo turned to her, a frightened look in his eyes. "It means the dam is failing."

"Failing?" asked Cam. "You mean it could burst?"

Neo nodded.

Cam took a deep breath. "But, if the dam breaks, all that water will come flooding into Lexis City. Everyone is in danger! Neo, we have to help!"

"We?" Neo said. "I can't do anything."

Cam faced Neo. "You can control water! Come with me to the dam."

"No," said Neo, shaking his head. "I won't be any use. I'll only make things worse."

"You don't know that! **Please, Neo!**" pleaded Cam. "My shape-shifting powers alone won't be enough to stop a flood. I can't do this by myself. I need your help."

Neo hesitated. "We won't get there in time."

"Yes, we will." Cam threw open the front door.

"Slink!" she yelled. "Call for back-up! The dam is failing! Follow me, Neo." She raced down the stairs and out into the street, spinning into her super suit. There, Switch took a deep breath, focused and changed into a horse.

"**WOW!**" exclaimed Neo. "That's amazing!"

The horse whinnied and twitched her head. Gingerly, Neo climbed up and held on tightly to her mane. Switch took off, galloping through the streets, past astonished pedestrians and drivers.

LEXIS CITY DAM

The Lexis City Dam helps control the flow of water from the river. It stops Lexis City from flooding. There is a reservoir – a large pool of water – behind the dam, which provides drinking water for the city.

5

CRACKS!

As they neared the dam, Switch and Neo could hear sirens and alarms wailing. A large crack had appeared in the huge wall, and smaller cracks were spreading out from it.

Neo slid off Switch's back. She trotted behind a big truck and transformed back into a human.

Neo and Cam stared up at the wall, which was creaking ominously. There were distant shouts from the workers at the dam, and a trickle of water ran down the wall.

"It's going to give way!" someone yelled from the top of the dam. "**EVACUATE!**"

Neo stepped back in shock. "That's my dad's voice! He's up there!"

People started running away from the dam.

"Neo," Cam said. "You have to hold back the water until the other heroes arrive."

Neo shook his head. "I ... I can't!"

Cam remembered what she had said to Axel earlier that day. "Close your eyes," she told Neo. "Breathe. Count to ten really slowly. It's just like the water you were controlling earlier. Trust yourself."

Neo closed his eyes and stretched out his hands towards the wall. "**One** ... **two** ... **three** ..." he began to count.

The trickle of water lifted off the wall. Droplets drifted through the air. Then they began to rise, back up to the cracks.

The wall **groaned** ... and then a whole section of the dam broke away, sending concrete slabs **crashing** to the ground.

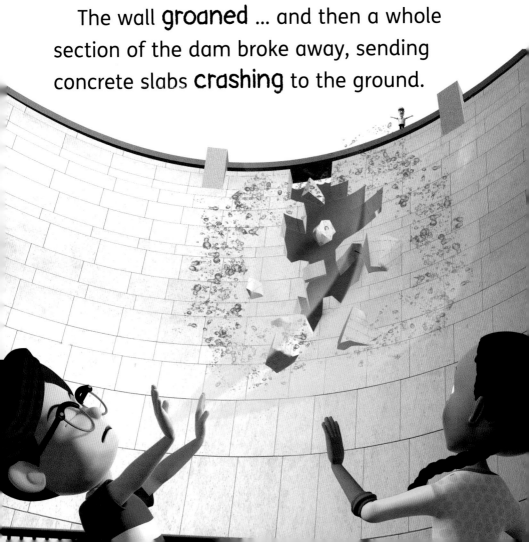

Cam flinched, expecting the water to come flooding out, but it stayed where it was, as if being held by an invisible wall.

"You're doing it!" she whispered to Neo. "You're holding it back!"

Sweat broke out on Neo's forehead.
His arms began to tremble.
"There's so much of it!"
he panted.
"So ... heavy!"

65

Cam knew Neo couldn't hold it for long. What could she do? Desperately, she looked around. Then she saw Nisha, in her Nimbus super suit, running towards them.

"**Keep going!**" Nimbus yelled at Neo. "**You're doing brilliantly!**" She stopped next to him and reached her arms up, too. Instantly, clouds started to gather over the dam, and the temperature fell rapidly.

"I can freeze it!" she said.

"**Coming through!**" shouted a voice. Pip, in her Boost super suit, raced to the break in the dam. She started lifting the heavy stones, piling them up against the dam to strengthen it.

Meanwhile, ice crystals spread across the water, hardening it into a solid wall.

Neo's arms finally gave way and he collapsed to the ground!

"You did it, Neo!" Cam cried. "I knew you could!" She heard footsteps behind her. She looked round but couldn't see anyone. Then Axel, dressed as Invisiboy, appeared next to her.

"What can I do?" he asked.

Cam suggested that Invisiboy go and switch all the alarms off so the engineers would know that it was safe to come back.

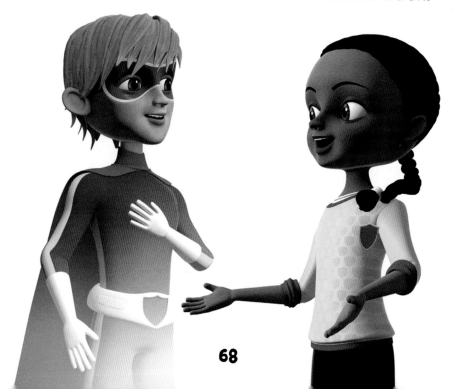

Just then, Neo's dad came running down the steps of the dam towards them. **"Neo! You're a hero!"** he said.

"Me?" said Neo.

"Of course!" Cam replied. "Now, come and meet my friends."

Everyone shook Neo's hand, and his dad led a round of cheering.

Neo felt so proud he lifted a hand into the air and sent a jet of water up like a fountain. It sprinkled tiny rainbow droplets on to everyone below.

"**Awesome** work, Neo," said Invisiboy. "Is it true you're coming to our school?"

Neo looked at his dad. Then he looked at Cam, who was smiling. "Yes," he said, taking a deep breath. "Yes, I am."